THE CHRISTIAN
TO TH

THE CHRISTIAN APPROACH TO THE JEW

by

H. L. ELLISON

Author of
*Men Spake from God: Studies in the Hebrew Prophets;
Ezekiel: the Man and his Message; Through Tragedy to
Triumph: A Study in the Book of Job; The Centrality of
the Messianic Idea for the Old Testament;* Contributor
to *The Church and the Jewish People.*

An " Edinburgh House Press " Book

Published by

LUTTERWORTH PRESS

LONDON

First published 1958
Sixth impression 1970

Copyright © 1958 Edinburgh House Press

ISBN 0 7188 1158 5

MADE AND PRINTED IN GREAT BRITAIN BY
MORRISON AND GIBB LIMITED, LONDON AND EDINBURGH

CHRISTIAN APPROACH SERIES

GENERAL INTRODUCTION

The great religions of the world are in encounter with each other as never before. People move swiftly; news and views travel in a matter of seconds; films and television give us an intimacy with people of all nations.

Religions have been stimulated to new life by nationalism and the desire of statesmen of countries newly independent to find a basis of unity and a source of inspiration for their independent existence.

People everywhere are conscious that the world is in a mess. The followers of this or that faith are eager to prove that their religion can direct the world to sanity and peace; other men, despairing of traditional beliefs, hope to solve the world's problems through Communism or through education and humanism.

It is not only in the countries of origin that the religions of Asia are exercising their missionary dynamic. We in the West may be tested by an encounter with Buddhism, Islam or Hinduism as representatives of these faiths come to our shores.

In other parts of the world Animism, the religion of primitive man, is still strong, often stronger than the faiths by which it is overlaid.

This series of short books is intended to give an objective and sympathetic account of other religions with a view to promoting deeper understanding of them. The writers will try to indicate the particular relevance of Christianity to each, how in fact the Gospel of Jesus Christ is good news in reference to the ultimate value of a particular faith. There will be no attempt to evade the challenge to Christians of these other religions—in thought, interpretation or living.

All religions ask fundamental questions about man, the universe in which he lives, his origin, purpose and end; his need of forgiveness and strength; his attempt to live the good life; his desire to get on terms with whatever final reality there may be; his longing for immortality. These questions are matters of life and death. In stressing the vital importance of religion, it is hoped that these books will be read by men of many faiths, and that they will find in them both truth and charity.

CONTENTS

General Introduction	5
Author's Foreword	7
I. Who is a Jew?	11
II. Two Thousand Five Hundred Years of History	15
III. Rabbinic Judaism	22
IV. The Modern Jew	29
V. The State of Israel	38
VI. The Jew and Jesus	44
VII. The Jew and I	50
Glossary	55
Statistics—1927 and 1957	60
Books for Further Reading	61

AUTHOR'S FOREWORD

THE operative word in the title of this little book is *Jew*. In other works in this series the stress is likely to be on systems of faith and thought, here it is on men and women. This is inevitable, for I am less concerned with Jews in general than with those we are likely to meet. The barrier between us and them is less a matter of religion and more of history. They share with us the Old Testament and its outlook on life. They speak the same language and share the same culture. If we find difficulty in understanding them and being friends with them, it will be mainly due to the past history of the relationship of the Christian world to Jewry.

Among the western, modern Jews we are all likely to meet, and, if we wish it, to count among our friends, Judaism is only one of the factors which determine their outlook on life and Christianity. My wish to be fair and practical has meant that I have had to look at all these factors and not least at the age-old sin of Christendom against the Jews. Inevitably, this has meant that my picture of Judaism is so incomplete as to be almost a travesty. I trust that the list of books for further reading may in measure remedy this (see p. 61). The Glossary may be a slight help too.

Some may take it ill that I descend to the plane of the individual in the last chapter. The Church can only hope that Jewry will accept her Lord, if she becomes a changed Church, and that must begin with the individual, not with resolutions of committees and synods. In addition, it has been the individual contact of the individual Jew with the individual Christian down the centuries that has convinced Jewry that Christianity is not good enough, and it is only a changed experience of individuals that will convince him of the contrary. Though Judaism is before all a community religion, it stresses before all else the actions of the individual in the community.

Before the expert takes his magnifying glass to my work, I would confess that for the sake of the general picture I have simplified and generalized. I trust that in spite of minor inaccuracy the general picture is correct.

I would assure my Jewish reader that I have done my utmost to be fair and objective. If he thinks I have failed, I shall welcome his rebuke and a sympathetic understanding of the difficulties that beset me.

Should this come into the hands of one who thinks that penitence for past crimes against Jewry or respect for the nobility of Judaism should restrain the Christian from sharing his Lord with the Jew, I would quote the words of Schalom Ben-Chorin, one of the best known of the Liberal Jews of Israel, from his public reply to an attack by the Rabbinate on Christian missions in Israel, " By its very nature Christianity is a religion that must carry on missionary work . . . The Church ceases to be the Church when it ceases to obey the command of its Lord : Go ye into all the world and preach the Gospel to every creature."

It is impossible at the present time to present the facts surrounding the setting up of the State of Israel in a manner that will be regarded as impartial by all concerned. Hence, I have been urged to avoid any but the most general mention of them. Since, however, it has not been merely the setting up of the State, but the manner in which it was set up that has deeply influenced the Jews of the world, and the problems of the State have become in measure the concern of Jews everywhere, it has been impossible to follow this advice. I have, however, sought to be as impartial as possible.

H. L. ELLISON

I

WHO IS A JEW?

WHO, or if you prefer it, what, is a Jew? There is a very widespread superstition abroad that the Jew is in certain ways a being apart, and that he is immediately recognizable.

It is quite likely that your own experience has shown you how wrong is this idea. It may be that you have worked beside someone for years without realizing that he was a Jew, until some chance remark or happening opened your eyes. On the other hand, you may always have taken for granted that someone was a Jew because of his face or accent until you discovered one day that he could have satisfied even a German Nazi, that he was of purest 'Aryan' origin.

But it is not only you and I who make these mistakes. In spite of frequent denials, there are thousands of anti-Semites who look on Charlie Chaplin, the film star, or Lord Montague Norman, for so many years governor of the Bank of England, as Jews. I can still remember the gasp of incredulous astonishment when I told a man, no friend of the Jews, that Harold Abrahams, at that time British sprint champion and Olympic title holder, was a Jew; even the name had never suggested this to him. On the other hand, there are many thousands of simple Christians who have never realized that Jesus Christ, the Virgin Mary, the Twelve Apostles and Paul were all Jews.

To say that the Jew is a descendant of the Jews of the

Old Testament does not take us very far. What we now call race had never very much meaning in Bible times. Joseph's wife was a high-born Egyptian. Moses was married to a Midianitess. Caleb, though a Kenite or a Kenezite, was accepted as one of the leaders of Judah. There was much intermarriage with the conquered Canaanites. The story of Ruth shows how easy it was to be 'naturalized'; apparently the one condition was the acceptance of the God of Israel. At the court of David we find foreigners like Uriah and Shawsha the Scribe in high positions. Is. 56 : 1–8 suggests that during the exile not a few heathen were won for the worship of the God of Israel. When the Jews returned from exile, their very existence as a people was for a time threatened by intermarriage, as we see from the vigorous reaction of Ezra and Nehemiah. Under the Maccabean kings, the Edomites and Galileans were made Jews by force. In the Roman world, until Christianity proved more attractive, Judaism drew many of the heathen into its fold. Even in the Middle Ages a whole Tartar tribe was converted to Judaism.

As a result of all this mixture there is no Jewish type. Some are indistinguishable from the Arab, others have the fair hair and blue eyes of the Scandinavian, yet others have Negro characteristics. In the east of Europe red hair was commonly taken as evidence of Jewish origin, while a 'Jewish nose' might just as well belong to an Armenian. The 'typical characteristics' mentioned in many older books were merely the results of the semi-starvation and congestion of the Jewish districts in Eastern Europe and are seldom to be found in younger Jews today. If you could be dropped in Tel-Aviv or Haifa, virtually completely Jewish cities, without know-

WHO IS A JEW?

ing where you were, you would say, "There are many Jews here", not, "This is a Jewish city".

Still less can we define a Jew by a common culture, religion or language. Apart from those who intend to settle there, there are few Jews outside the State of Israel who can speak Hebrew fluently; most of the exceptions have learnt it for religious purposes. Though fifty years ago it might have been said that a majority of Jews understood Yiddish (basically a German dialect), today it is a dying language, and the average Jew outside Israel speaks and thinks in the language of the country where he is a citizen.

In the Middle Ages everyone in Central and Western Europe, apart from the Jews, had to accept the authority of the Pope and seldom thought of the possibility of doing anything else. Similarly, until the end of the Jewish 'Middle Ages', which did not come until about 1800, virtually all Jews followed the teaching of Rabbinic Judaism. Since then the strict adherents of this form of Judaism have become a minority of the people, and a wide variety of belief or no-belief can be found. There are probably as many Jews who would declare themselves atheists or agnostics as those who can be considered strictly Orthodox. For a high proportion nationalism has taken the place of, or assumed priority over, religion.

Outside the religious sphere we cannot find a Jewish culture. Whether it is music, art, drama or literature, it is impossible to find anything secular that can be called typically Jewish. The Jew has always been prepared, once he admitted a secular side to life, to accept the culture of the majority among whom he has lived. Even the State of Israel has produced nothing typical in these fields, for it is still too young. But even if we could find something indubitably Jewish in the cultural sphere, it would not be common to all Jews. Between the highly cultured Jew of Western Europe and the downtrodden Jews of the Yemen and the Atlas Mountains there is culturally as great a gap as between us and the poverty-stricken Arab *fellahin*.

Who is a Jew? Not even the Jew can give a satisfactory definition, and the State of Israel has carefully avoided committing itself. The verdict in the Rufeisen (Father Daniel) case before the High Court early in 1963 affirmed merely that a Jew who adopted another religion (by which we can understand Christianity) could not be regarded as a Jew. The fact is that Jews exist, whether we can define a Jew or not. To understand this we must know a little Jewish history.

II

TWO THOUSAND FIVE HUNDRED YEARS OF HISTORY

JERUSALEM fell to Nebuchadnezzar in 586 B.C. From then, apart from the short period of the Maccabean kings (140–63 B.C.), until the State of Israel was set up in 1948, the Jews lived everywhere under foreign domination. Furthermore, at no time in this long period did Palestine contain the majority of the Jews, even as it does not today. At times it had a sizable Jewish population; at times this dwindled to virtually nothing. Only in Peki'in, a little village off the beaten track in Upper Galilee, is there a tradition of a continuous Jewish community from Roman times down to our own days. Here it is not possible to give more than an outline of the high lights of this long period.

In the Persian period (538–333 B.C.) the Jewish community in Palestine was confined to a small area around Jerusalem and was overshadowed by its neighbours. The major community was in Babylonia, from which most of the exiles had not returned. Hebrew, except for religious purposes, was largely abandoned for Aramaic.

After the conquests of Alexander the Great (died 323 B.C.) Jews spread rapidly along the coasts of the Mediterranean and into the main inland trading centres. This westward dispersion spoke Greek, not Aramaic, and was mainly urban, in contrast to the farmers of Palestine and Babylonia. Its chief centre was Alexandria in

Egypt; some hundred thousand Jews lived in two of the five districts of the city and enjoyed a large measure of self-government. Here we find the first traces of that hatred of the Jews which has had such tragic results down the centuries until it reached its climax in our day in Hitler's anti-Semitism.

Alexander's conquests meant the introduction of Greek language and culture to Asia and North-East Africa. Hellenism, as this transplanted culture is called, spread rapidly and was steadily influencing the Jews, when Antiochus Epiphanes (175–164 B.C.), ruler in Syrian Antioch over a crumbling kingdom, stretching from the Mediterranean and Asia Minor to the frontiers of India and Egypt, made its acceptance a matter of state policy. The dedication of the Temple in Jerusalem to Greek gods in 168 B.C. and the prohibition of basic Jewish religious customs led to a heroic rebellion. Against all expectations, this led to victory and freedom (140 B.C.) under the Maccabean priest-kings. By 76 B.C. the frontiers of the Jewish state had practically reached and at some points passed the traditional Biblical limits of Dan to Beersheba.

Unfortunately, the unwise rule of these kings created serious internal tensions, and as soon as Rome appeared on the scene (63 B.C.) the state collapsed. Roman rule hastened the spread of Jews westward, and they received many privileges.

The next two centuries, into which falls the life of Jesus, were a time of the most fanatical expectation of the Messiah. The resulting opposition to both the Herods and the Romans led to the steady grinding down of Palestine and cost the lives of at least two hundred thousand of her best sons. The climax came in the seventy years from A.D. 64. In 70 the Temple was destroyed, and according to Josephus over a million were killed in Jerusalem alone. In A.D. 115–117 the Jewish dispersion in Mesopotamia, Egypt, Cyrene and Cyprus was nearly wiped out. The last desperate resistance of Judea came in 132–135. When it was over, another half million had lost their lives and Jewish slaves were a drug in the market. From then till our own times Jews were a minority in Palestine.

For a time the spiritual centre of Jewry remained in Galilee, but from the time of Constantine, the rising supremacy of Christianity made its continuance increasingly difficult, and so the leadership of Jewry passed to the community in Babylonia. In Europe the Jew rapidly came to occupy the position of a second-class citizen. Already early in the seventh century the Jews of Spain and France were given the choice of baptism or expulsion, a choice which was to become bitterly frequent in later centuries.

In Babylonia, after some centuries of prosperity, the community was crippled by persecution on the part of the Persian rulers. It revived for a time after the Muslim conquest, but before long its glory passed to the Jews who entered Spain at the heels of the Arab conquerors. Here too in the twelfth century Muslim fanaticism faced them with the choice of Islam or flight.

The Crusades are the next great landmark in Jewish memory. The First Crusade, proclaimed in 1095, let loose men's passions, and it was always easier to plunder and murder Jews than to fight Muslims. Metz, the towns on the Rhine, Prague, Salonica, all saw their Jewish communities butchered, and the capture of Jerusalem was celebrated by the massacre of all Jews in it. In later crusades the wave of Jew-baiting spread ever wider, and in 1189 England was involved.

To make matters worse, the Jews were accused from this time on of murdering Christians, especially children, to use their blood in their religious ceremonies. Fire and plague, notably the Black Death, were also attributed to them. As a result, even where they were prosperous, a continual threat hung over them. There was a growing tendency to force them to wear a distinguishing badge and to live in clearly defined portions of the towns (the ghetto).

In 1290 the Jews of England had the choice of conversion or expulsion—over 16,000 left the land. The turn of the 100,000 of France came next. The expulsion order was given in 1306, but there was constant vacillation by the kings until 1394, when the order was made final. Many of those who had returned in the interval were massacred by the shepherds of Southern France, and their actions were copied in Northern Spain. European Jewry was largely saved by its friendly reception in Poland, where, in spite of occasional massacres, it was reasonably treated and granted a considerable measure of self-government.

Spanish Jewry had gradually become prosperous again, but it came under increasing pressure, and in 1391 a wave of massacres claimed over 70,000 victims. For the only time in this long history of persecution, there were a large number of outward conversions to Christianity (the Marranos). The guilty conscience of the persecutor and the frequent insincerity of the convert led to a steady worsening of the position of the Marranos, and in 1478 the Inquisition—later to turn its attention to others suspected of heresy—began its horrid work among them.

In 1492 the Jews were expelled from Spain and over 150,000 preferred exile to swelling the number of the Marranos. In 1496 Portugal followed Spain's example, with the added brutality that many Jews, especially children, were baptized by force.

The steadily improving position of the Jews in the great commercial centres of North-Western Europe in the seventeenth century was more than offset by the deterioration of the situation in Poland. From 1648 Cossack and Russian attacks on Poland were accompanied by large-scale massacres of the Jews, the worst being that of 1768. In addition, there was a serious drop in religious hopes with the collapse of Sabbatai Zevi (1626–1676), the last of the pseudo-Messiahs who had sporadically appeared in Jewry.

The Jewish communities of Western Europe gradually acquired security and political rights, especially during the course of last century, while their numbers were steadily augmented by fugitives from the East. The partitions of Poland ushered in a century and a half of utmost suffering for those Jews, the majority, who found themselves under Russian rule. They were first confined to the former Polish provinces (the Pale of Settlement), which was steadily reduced in size. For about a quarter of a century their children, as young as eight, were conscripted for twenty-five years' military service. After a short period of relaxation, a wave of massacres broke out in 1881, which added the word pogrom to our vocabulary. Though these ended the following year, the authorities followed them by savage restrictive laws, which continued in force until the collapse of Czarist rule. Pobiedonotsev, the Procurator of the Holy Synod, said openly that the Jewish problem in Russia would be solved by the conversion of one-third, the emigration of another, and the extermination of the remainder. It was in this period that the mass emigration began which has made the Jewish community in the United States the largest in the world.

The pogroms turned the thoughts of some to Palestine, and this feeling was reinforced by the outbreak of anti-Semitism in Germany in 1879, which soon had its supporters throughout Europe and forced many Jews to question whether they had any future in European society. The two streams coalesced in the Zionist movement, which held its first congress in 1897. The Balfour Declaration of 1917 and the British Mandate over Palestine in 1920 transformed Zionism from a minority movement to the greatest force within Jewry.

In the troubled years between the wars the Jew was increasingly made the scapegoat by anti-Semites for all the troubles of the world, including Communism, in spite of the fact that Jewish leaders in the U.S.S.R. were being steadily liquidated. The world found it hard to believe that Hitler meant his anti-Semitism seriously, and for the most part looked on incredulously as the million Jews of Germany, Austria and Czechoslovakia were robbed, humiliated and tortured. Realization came too late to save the majority by a relaxation in immigration regulations. With the outbreak of war the Nazis were freed from all inhibitions. The details of their cruelty are too terrible for publication, and the Jews were their chief victims. Of the less than seven million under their shadow, by their over-running of Eastern Europe, six million perished under conditions of the most revolting cruelty.

It was the presence of the survivors, broken in body

and unwilling to continue living in lands that had become a nightmare to them, which moved the United Nations to agree in principle to the partition of Palestine, and this led in turn to the setting up of the State of Israel (14th May, 1948). A year of heroic fighting against a league of six Arab states guaranteed the reality of the new state.

Part, then, of the heritage that makes a Jew is the memory of Nebuchadnezzar and Rome, the Crusades and the Inquisition, the ghetto and the Jew-badge, the pogroms and Hitler's concentration camps. But to survive such a history an inner power was needed and this must be sought in the Jewish religion.

III

RABBINIC JUDAISM

VIRTUALLY all who have written about the Jews have agreed that their religion was the chief power that preserved their national existence in spite of dispersion, landlessness and persecution. To understand this, we must find those elements in the religion which gave it this power and also preserved Jewry from the attractions of Christianity and Islam, both of which claim to represent the true spirit of the Old Testament revelation.

Personally, I think that the sense of having been chosen by God is the most powerful element in Judaism. This belief was firmly anchored in the history of the Exodus and the Conquest of Canaan, and it had been confirmed by the return from exile. But though this has led to a feeling of being different, it has seldom produced that sense of superiority that has so often been a marked characteristic of the more powerful nations of the world.

The Jew has been kept from this false sense of superiority by another element in his religion, his realization of the absolute morality and goodness of God. For many nations their power was the proof of their election, for the Jew it has rather been his preservation in the midst of suffering and oppression, while at the same time he has regarded these as evidence for the sin of his people and for the inflexible righteousness of God, which will not show favouritism to His elect but expects more rather than less from them (cf. Amos 3 : 2).

RABBINIC JUDAISM

The Jew considers his special privilege to be that God has given him a full, perfect and final revelation of His will in the Law of Moses; for the Orthodox Jew his supreme glory is not political power or wealth, but the keeping of this Law. This is the most obvious feature of Rabbinic Judaism;[1] it derives its dynamic from the conception of God's character and of the relationship of the Jew to God.

A Jew reading this would probably say that the most important element of all, the absolute unity of God, has been omitted. A Judaism without monotheism, the monotheism of the Old Testament, would be unthinkable and a contradiction in terms. But the standard formulation of that monotheism in so much of Judaism[2] is far more a defensive bulwark against Christianity than an original and dynamic feature of Jewish faith.

The Jew speaks of God's Torah, and it is regrettable that we have through the influence of the 2nd century B.C. Greek translation (the Septuagint) come to render it as the Law. The element of law is certainly in Torah, but it means above all Instruction. The Torah exists not merely to be kept as an end in itself, but that through the keeping of it men might come to know God better.

Many of those who returned from Babylonia to the ruins of Jerusalem and the ravaged hills of Judea were

[1] For the use of Orthodox in relation to Judaism see special note at the end of the chapter.

[2] E.g. "I believe with perfect faith that the Creator, blessed be his Name, is a unity, and that there is no Unity in any manner like unto his, and that he alone is our God, who was, is, and will be." (The Second of the Thirteen Principles of the Faith by Maimonides, to be found in any Jewish Prayer Book.) This formulation is not binding on the Rabbinic Jew, but it will have been only the rarest exception that will not have accepted it.

priests whose hearts were set on the restoration of the Temple and its sacrifices. Others represented those who had learnt in exile to regard it as God's punishment for the failure of the people as a whole to keep God's law. Ezra seems to have been the man who really initiated the drive to bring the Torah to the common man. In the four centuries between Ezra and Jesus every effort was made to see that the Jewish boy learnt it (this was the main motive behind the very high level of Jewish literacy in the 1st century A.D.) and kept it.

Though those committed to a hundred per cent loyalty to the Torah were in a minority in the time of Jesus—they were represented by groups like the Pharisees and the Qumran Covenanters—they had won the respect, if not always the obedience, of the common people and were frequently able to enforce their views on the priestly rulers. After the collapse of nationalistic hopes in the grim years between A.D. 64–135, the descendants of the Pharisees were able, after a struggle lasting about a century, to make their concept of the keeping of the Torah virtually coterminous with Judaism and Jewry. The centre of community life became the synagogue, and the rabbi [1] the leader of the community.

The rabbis, regarding the Pentateuch not simply as a law book but as Divine Instruction, deduced from it principles and laws which would cover the whole of life. These principles and the laws deduced from them, together with certain customs of immemorial antiquity,

---

[1] The rabbi must not be compared with a Christian minister. He is not a priest, leader of worship or a preacher; he need not even be a pastor. He is an expert in the Torah, its teacher and expounder. In the modern synagogue, under the influence of Christian surroundings, he may be expected to carry out some of the functions of the Christian minister, but these remain strictly secondary.

form the Oral Law in contrast to the Written Law, i.e. the Pentateuch, and both are regarded as having equal authority, and the two together form the Torah of the Rabbinic Jew. Indeed, it is considered that the Oral Law was, in germ at least, given to Moses at Sinai. The formulation of the Oral Law is found in the Mishnah (c. A.D. 200), while its clarification and detailed application are given by the Gemara, virtually completed by A.D. 500. The two together form the Talmud. Any one who wishes really to understand the methods of rabbinic exegesis needs to be familiar as well with the *Midrashim* (sing. *Midrash*), the official commentaries on the Old Testament, which date from about the same time as the Talmud.

For us the outstanding peculiarity of the rabbinic treatment of the Torah is that after establishing what commandments exist—they say there are 613, 365 of which are negative and 248 positive—they surrounded them with a ' fence ', i.e. subsidiary enactments intended to guarantee the keeping of the fundamental laws. While the original 613 commandments are immutable, the fence is theoretically changeable, though in fact it is questionable whether any means exists today to modify it, which the Orthodox would generally accept.

Obviously, much in the Talmud is wearisome to the ordinary reader, and there is much in its twenty-five closely printed folio volumes that looks like hair-splitting ; the same is true of any comprehensive and detailed legal treatise. Those portions that are generally held up to ridicule or worse by anti-Semites are mostly those stories and rules that represent the outlook and superstitions of the period of its compilation. They have no binding authority on the Orthodox and can be easily paralleled by the Lives of the Saints and pious legends from the Middle Ages.

It goes without saying that there were Jews who were caught up in the sheer intellectual joy of casuistic hair-splitting and that others became mere legalists, keeping the Law merely for the sake of future reward. Neither attitude is typical of Rabbinic Judaism at its best, and they can be paralleled in all developed religions including Christianity. The stress of the rabbis is that the law must be kept out of devotion to God, not for the sake of its keeper. God being righteous, the Jew expected his reward, but only because he had acted for God's sake, who had privileged him by giving him the Torah.

The essential sanity of rabbinic legislation behind its detailed casuistry is seen in the ruling that to save his life the Jew might break any commandment in the Law except those against murder, unchastity and idolatry. The rabbis stressed that the purpose of God's revelation was to give *life*, and they did not encourage needless martyrdom.

The tendency to legalism was constantly countered by the influence of mysticism, which has played a great role in Rabbinic Judaism from at least the 2nd century A.D. In a brief work like this I must content myself with the mention of Kabbalism with its chief work, *The Zohar* (c. 1280), and of Chassidism, founded by Baal Shem-Tov (died 1760), which popularized mysticism among the Jewish masses of Eastern Europe, and thereby revitalized the Judaism of his day, which seemed in danger of losing itself in legalism.

Judaism has no sacraments. Its festivals are memorials of God's acts in the past, while the impressive fast of Yom Kippur (Day of Atonement) reminds the Jew that however carefully he may have kept the Law, he is ultimately dependent as individual and people on the forgiving grace of God. The morning and evening services of the synagogue are merely those fixed prayers which the Orthodox Jew is under obligation to repeat twice a day, preferably in the fellowship of the community. The Sabbath morning service has the reading of the Law as its centre.

I can best end this chapter by a quotation from the Mishnah : " These are the things for which no measure is prescribed (i.e. the more the better): the corners of the field (Lev. 23 : 22), First-fruits (Deut. 26 : 1–11), the Festal Offering (Deut. 16 : 16, 17), deeds of loving-kindness and the study of the Law (*Peah* i. 1)."

Additional Note

ORTHODOX JUDAISM

The terms 'Orthodox Judaism' and 'Orthodoxy' are in general use among Jews, but their use is misleading. The term Orthodoxy is really a Christian one and derives from the conflicts in the early Church over the doctrines of the Trinity, the Nature of Christ, the Atonement, etc. Jewish theology is so much simpler than Christian that some writers have erroneously suggested that it does not even exist. Down the centuries there were seldom cases where the great fundamental principles of Judaism were challenged ; controversy was more likely to be centred in how the Law was kept ; and where it was kept according to rabbinic precept, it was assumed that the underlying theological truths were accepted. Hence, when we are thinking of the historic development of Judaism, 'Rabbinic Judaism' is a better term.

The term Orthodox only became suitable last century, when under the influence of modern thought the divine origin and authority of the Torah were challenged. But even here it has been suggested that Orthopraxy (i.e. doing rightly) would be a better term than Orthodoxy. Recently even the term Fundamentalist has been introduced to designate the old-fashioned Orthodox.

Anyone reading *The Jewish Chronicle*, the semi-official weekly of British Jewry, will soon realize that there is no generally accepted standard of orthodoxy. The more inflexible upholders of tradition deny the orthodoxy of the laxer, but they are unable to enforce their views and practices.

IV

THE MODERN JEW

WHILE the Church was gradually adapting its medieval modes of thinking to the challenge of the Renaissance, the French Revolution and the modern scientific age, Jewry was for the most part continuing in the old mental and spiritual moulds. The new age only became real for most of West European Jewry during or after the French Revolution, because political restrictions and rabbinic conservatism had combined to exclude the new influences moving Europe since the Renaissance. It was the Russian pogroms that broke down the old barriers in Eastern Europe, while for many of the Jews in Muslim lands, it needed their transportation to the State of Israel to awaken them to the modern world.

Had the transition been more gradual, it may well be that Rabbinic Judaism would have had time to adapt itself to the new world in which it found itself. As it was, the network of rules and regulations that covered the whole of life proved irrelevant for so much in the world in which we live; on the other hand, new circumstances were met for which there was no legislation. Above all, the granting of full civil rights with their accompanying responsibilities, especially military service, repeatedly made the keeping of many of the most cherished ritual practices almost impossible. Exactly as with non-Jews, very many allowed themselves to be carried away by the secular spirit of the age, and either forgot their religion or relegated it to second place in their lives. Those who sought to remain true to the past for the most part withdrew themselves from the world around them.

The Orthodox

You are not likely to meet a truly Orthodox Jew. Their number is relatively small, and many of them think they can only preserve their orthodoxy by avoiding contacts with non-Jews as far as is practicable. Very many of them are strongly influenced by Chassidism and its mystical teaching. Though this does not make light of the keeping of the Law, it places a joyful devotion to God far above it. In addition, its adherents place great reliance on their rabbis or *tzaddikim*, who are valued for their spiritual gifts rather than their Talmudic knowledge and are considered to be mediators between their followers and God.

Another factor militating against Orthodoxy today is the Rabbinic ideal of Talmudic study. Every man was expected within the limits of his capabilities to devote all his spare time to the study of the Torah. The strident claims of the modern world on our time and its subtle drawing of our affections leave the average Jew with little time for these studies. Experience shows that where Rabbinic Judaism has become second-hand, it has always lost its grip on man's devotion.

The setting up of the State of Israel has been a serious blow for Orthodoxy. It is not so much that the majority of the leaders of the State have little love for it; it is rather that experience has shown that many of the rabbinic laws are incapable of enforcement and even of being kept in this modern Jewish state. They were developed and codified in completely different circumstances and they presuppose a community in which the religious authorities are dominant. They make no allowance for the modern secular state.

The 'Conservative'

Many of the Jews of Britain and America would call themselves Orthodox, but a fairer name would be 'Conservative', a term actually in use in America. Few of them unquestioningly accept the divine authority of the Torah and in practice keep as much of it as they consider reasonable for the conditions under which they live. Many of them are prepared to confess quite openly that they keep the ritual demands of the Law, in contrast to the moral, merely because they are part of their being Jews, not because they consider them divine commandments.

Even among the strictly Orthodox there have been the possibilities of stricter and laxer interpretations of the Law, and it was always recognized, at least in theory, that rigour was not necessarily a sign of spirituality. There is a far wider degree of observance or non-observance among the 'Conservatives', and it is even less a pointer to the faith of the individual. In contrast to the Orthodox they are normally glad of social and religious contacts with their non-Jewish neighbours, though the stricter among them will find it difficult to accept an invitation to a common meal.

The Liberal

Early in the nineteenth century the spirit of the age led to the founding of 'Reform' synagogues, first in Germany, then in Britain and other European countries, and also somewhat later in America. The stress of the Reform movement varied from country to country. In Britain it was the repudiation of rabbinic authority. The Written Law was set above the Oral Law. While the latter was not rejected completely, only as much was retained as was considered to have spiritual value. Though the Conservative would probably deny it, the Reform Jew is doing deliberately and systematically what many Conservative Jews do haphazardly.

Because the Reform synagogue in this sense occupied a sort of halfway house, it never became very influential, particularly as many of the laxer Conservative synagogues came to occupy almost the same position. The same spirit, however, which queried the inspiration and authority of the Oral Law, passed on to query those of the Written Law. The resultant faith is known as Reform Judaism in America, but in Britain, probably more suitably, as Liberal Judaism.

The Liberal Jew follows the dominant school of modern Old Testament scholars and lays his chief stress on the Prophets, not on the Law. His faith is typical modern liberal humanism and differs but little from that of his counterpart in the Church, the more so as he normally has a deep respect for the character and teaching of Jesus. Were it not that the Liberal synagogue has kept certain customs from the past, either out of sentimentality, or because they enshrine spiritual truths for the worshipper, it would be difficult to distinguish its worship from that of the Unitarians.

In America the Liberal (Reform) movement, in spite of a Conservative and even Orthodox revival, is probably dominant. In Britain it is much weaker in numbers, but enjoys high respect for the spiritual sincerity of many of its members, as well as for their intellectual and social standing.

The Secularist

The same forces that, during the last century, have separated the urban masses of Western Europe from the Church have been equally powerful within Jewry. It is probable that there is a higher proportion of synagogue membership among the Jews of Britain than there is of church membership among comparable social groups among their non-Jewish neighbours. This is not to be attributed to the greater strength of Judaism, but rather that, for many of them, the synagogue is the only means by which they can express their Jewishness. It is his religion that has kept the Jew a Jew down the centuries, and even if the modern Jew loses his religion, he feels he cannot break with it entirely. In addition, the Synagogue's stress on actions rather than a creed frees them from an outward conformity to a form of faith they do not sincerely share. In spite of its proportionately higher numbers, the Synagogue has probably been more seriously affected than the Church.

Extreme secularism has the same results the world over. Jewry has its representatives in the criminal classes, both among the small fry and those known to the police of the world. Their background shows itself, however, in the fact that the proportion of Jews convicted for the more brutal crimes, e.g. murder, rape and assault, is much lower than might be expected from their numbers. Unless he has completely detached himself from his people, the Jewish secularist is normally more influenced by memories of the Synagogue than the non-Jewish by those of the Church.

The Idealist

This influence of the past is seen in the very high proportion of humanistic idealists among non-religious Jews. They are frequently generous donors to those Christian efforts which they consider to be of value to the community at large. Though the divine authority of the Law has been rejected, they still recognize its abiding validity where doing good to their fellow-men is concerned.

This explains why so many Jews are supporters of the parties of the Left, a fact so often interpreted by the anti-Semite as a proof of a Jewish plot against society.

In the ghettoes of Eastern Europe at the end of last century only the exceptional man could find a middle way between Rabbinic Judaism and atheism. At no time in its history had Jewry been reduced to such abject poverty and misery, and it seemed to many of the young people that the rabbis were fostering and supporting a type of society pledged to the preservation of things as they were. For them Marxism, with its promise of a new earth in which dwelleth righteousness, came with all the glory of a gospel. This vision sustained thousands of them in the miseries of the slums of New York and other eastern seaboard cities of America, where the mass immigration from Russia gradually adapted itself to the strange new world in which it found itself. Yet others were upborne in their efforts to rebuild their national home in Palestine by the dream of creating a new society as well. Whatever the future of the *kibbutz*,[1] the communal colony, in Israel, there can be little doubt that it is the one significant experiment in communal living that this century has seen.

[1] See p. 56.

It is easy to understand then that Jews figured prominently in the early days of Marxism and then of Communism. The removal of Kaganovitch from office in the U.S.S.R. (July 1957) does not merely represent the removal of the last Jew from any position of power in Russian Communism; it is also symbolic of the complete disillusionment of Jewry with Communism as it has worked out in practice. In Israel out of the 120 members of the Knesset only six are Communists, five of them being Arabs, and a high proportion of their support came from Arab voters.

The Nationalist

In Bible times the name Jew had both a religious and a national meaning. During the long centuries of Jewry's dispersion, though it was never forgotten that the Jews were a people, their existence was increasingly explained in purely religious terms. With the rise of modern liberalism, many Jews turned their backs on any national or racial connotation in the name. Indeed there was a period last century when the average West-European Jew made it his ambition to assimilate himself to those among whom he lived in everything except religion.

In the last twenty years of the century, however, it became increasingly and tragically clear that this policy was quite unavailing to check the rapidly running tide of anti-Semitism. A return to the old Orthodoxy was generally felt to be impossible and in its place we find a revival of national feeling. This was powerfully supported by the Jewish youth of Russia who had abandoned their religion in despair but who clung to nationalism as a means of maintaining their existence.

It was Theodore Herzl's book *Der Judenstaat* (1896) that gave expression to this new trend and it was followed in 1897 by the first Zionist Congress, which was held in Basle. The 204 delegates were not merely representative of world Jewry as a whole, but also opened the eyes of the western leaders of the new movement to the mass support they might expect from the younger Jews of Eastern Europe. On his return home, Herzl wrote in his diary: " If I were to sum up the Basle Congress in one word—which I shall not do openly—it would be this: at Basle I founded the Jewish State. If I were to say this today, I would be met by universal laughter. In five years, perhaps, and certainly in fifty, every one will see it."[1] On May 14, 1948, over three months before the fifty years of Herzl's prophecy had run their course, the Jewish State of Israel was proclaimed.

This half century was so filled with highest heroism and solid achievement that few Jews were not profoundly influenced by it. The Liberal might oppose Zionist nationalism on principle, but he could not help feeling a growing admiration for, and finally pride in, its fruits. The Orthodox gradually decreased their opposition and have today, with the exception of the small extreme group of the Naturei Kartei, been willing to accept the fruits of its success. Nationalism has become the effective religion of many, especially among the young, both inside and outside Israel. Though the Jewish masses of America and Britain may look on Israel as the home-land of any Jews but themselves, yet they find it increasingly impossible to remain aloof from its fate and prosperity.

It is fair to say, then, that if we want to understand

[1] Quoted in Israel Cohen: *A Short History of Zionism*, p. 47.

the Jew whom we meet, we must bear in mind the centuries of history that have helped to mould him, his religion or lack of it, which is inescapably influenced by the old Rabbinic Orthodoxy, and his attitude towards the new State of Israel, which cannot have left him unmoved.

V

THE STATE OF ISRAEL

THOUGH the joys and sorrows, the successes and failures of Israel do not belong, strictly speaking, to the subject of our little book, they are so linked up with the outlook of the modern Jew living in other lands that we must look at them briefly.

Once the failure of Bar Cochba's revolt had finally put an end to the hope of a Jewish state in Palestine it was the main effort of the rabbis to impress upon the Jews that they were not a nation like all other nations. Their neighbours took the rabbis at their word and through many centuries of persecution insisted on treating the Jews as essentially different beings. One of the main aims of Zionism was to end the widely prevailing hatred and suspicion of the Jews by making them a nation like all others; the chief means to this end was to be the setting up of a Jewish state.

Although it had been mainly Zionist vision and enterprise that had gradually built up the Jewish community in Palestine under the British Mandate, until its population reached about 660,000, Zionism was not strong enough to frame the new state in 1948 according to its ideals. Israel is a compromise. Though its most powerful element is modern secularism, which regards religion as a private affair, yet the orthodox rabbis have been able to maintain a firm footing in many sections of public life. Whether either side will ultimately triumph it is impossible to say. For the present the visitor finds a strange juxtaposition, sometimes harmonious, sometimes ludicrous, not seldom irksome. What is important is that this enforced compromise makes it possible for Jews throughout the world to look on Israel as truly Jewish, not merely as the expression of the views of a section of Jewry.

It is not only inside Israel that Zionism has failed to reach its full goal. Though the Jew finds that many, influenced by the heroism of the founders of Israel, treat him with a new respect, yet many of his old friends have grown cold because of the wrong they claim has been done to the Arabs. In addition, the traditional anti-Semite has found in the troubles that have gathered round Israel new fuel for his fires. Edward Atiyah is correct enough when he writes, " It is one of the tragic facts of modern history . . . that Jewish nationalism and Arab nationalism started about the same time, and the goal of the former could not be attained without bringing it into a mortal conflict with the latter in one of the most vital regions of the Arab world." [1]

There is a conflict of evidence as to whether the Zionist efforts before 1914 awakened any deep hostility among the Arabs of Palestine. The very doubt shows that there cannot have been much, but on the other hand the essentially secularist Zionist found it hard to believe that there would be sincere Muslim resentment at his presence, nor could he grasp how deeply his western outlook and habits might shock the conservative eastern society in which he now found himself.

The Jew cannot possibly be held responsible for the fact that Britain emerged from the war in 1918 burdened by completely irreconcilable promises. Indeed it is

[1] Edward Atiyah: *The Arabs*, p. 100.

doubtful whether the Cabinet itself realized how far the pressure of war had led it into contradictions in the Near East. Unfortunately, the Arabs of Palestine came to believe that the Jews were the sole reason why they did not receive full independence, and the Mandatory government made matters worse by alternatively trying conciliation and repression without any clear goal for its policy.[1] The Arab became emotionally incapable of appreciating the Jewish building-up of Palestine and the extent to which he himself was profiting from it. The secularized Zionist, on the other hand, was hampered by his Marxist blinkers and could not see the true cause of the enmity; as a result, only a minority group tried seriously to bridge the gulf between the two communities.

It may be that the two communities would ultimately have found one another in a common hostility to the Mandatory rule had Hitler not come to power in Germany in 1933. Jewish immigration into Palestine, which for six years had been running at an annual average of just over 5,000, rocketed at once to 30,000, 42,000, and finally 62,000 in 1935, before the authorities imposed even more drastic limitations on it, and by the White Paper of 1939 foreshadowed its complete termination. The period of illegal immigration began. The Arabs were shocked by the realization that a Jewish majority in the country had become a possibility, and they were embittered by the realization that the western world was putting up its shutters against the victims of Nazi persecution, until Palestine and Shanghai remained the only places of refuge.

Arab violence led to government repression, and this

[1] An impartial study of this very controversial subject will be found in James Parkes: *A History of Palestine*, chs. xv–xvii.

THE STATE OF ISRAEL

in turn led to Jewish terrorism, especially after the gates of Palestine were barred to those who were fleeing from Hitler's concentration camps and gas chambers. Britain's announcement early in 1947 that it was abandoning its Mandate was unexpected, but it was really the only course; though the manner of abandonment was calculated to cause the maximum of trouble.

It is doubtful whether the United Nations could have found a solution that would have satisfied both sides. With open eyes and the best of intentions, it adopted a plan which was bound to lead to bloodshed and misery but took not the least steps to avoid them until it was much too late; though owing to the policy of the British Government any effective action would have been very difficult.[1] It was far more the defeat of the Arab armies than the efforts of the Conciliation Committee of the United Nations that led to the armistice agreements of 1949, which are still in force. Since then the United Nations seem to have been far more interested in the maintenance of the *status quo* than in the creation of true peace. In addition, they have acquiesced in the exploitation of the Arab refugees as centres of growing hatred, instead of insisting that the millions poured out for their maintenance should be used constructively for their resettlement. The Arabs must bear the blame for very many of the half million refugees (a number that has greatly increased owing to the high birth rate among them), for the Arab High Command called on them to leave their homes when Israel was invaded. The number of those who obeyed was, however, swelled by those who fled in fear after the Jewish terrorist massacre at Deir Yussein, and minor incidents elsewhere.

[1] For a map of the frontiers proposed see Parkes *op. cit.* p. 329.

As a result of all this, Israel has to keep a large army ready and to spend a ruinous proportion of the national wealth on armaments, when its one desire is peacefully to build up the land and to put its shaky economy on a sound basis. The odium that has fallen on the Jew he finds particularly galling, for he finds himself the whipping-boy for what he considers the faults of others.

In another sphere too the Zionist has had to experience disappointment. The almost daemonic drive behind the earlier stages of the movement in Palestine expressed motives far deeper than the mere wish to build up a National Home. After centuries of being despised and rejected, the Zionist wished to show the world that he could restore his own land to fertility after so many centuries of neglect, instead of migrating to virgin fields, as did so many. Then too he wished to show that he could create a nobler society than that which had persecuted him and cast him out. Single-minded devotion to the building up of Zion, both of the land and of society, became the central motif of Zionist education.

So far as the land is concerned the apparently impossible has repeatedly been achieved so that today there are areas under cultivation which were probably waste land already in the time of Joshua. On the social side the chief fruit of Zionist idealism has been the communal settlement (the *kibbutz* or *kvutza*). Here all members are equal, and all work for the community, not for themselves. The goal of the community was not its own good and ultimate prosperity and ease, but the good of the people as a whole. Though the *kibbutz* was undoubtedly the answer to a particular situation—the Zionist resettlement could never have succeeded without it—it was also a major contribution to the social problems of modern society and was hailed by many leading sociologists. It was the younger generation brought up and trained in the communal colonies that was the major factor in Israel's incredible defeat of the Arab League.

Alas, in the day of victory Israel's ideal was found to have feet of clay. Many a *kibbutz* found it hard to subordinate its own interests to those of the new state. Some of the older members felt that they were now entitled to relax in an easier life, and even more of the younger longed for a fuller life than the small community could offer. Finally, when the quarrel between the two left-wing parties, Mapai and Mapam, came to a head—a quarrel with all the typical bitterness of Marxist quarrels and with all their apparent lack of adequate cause—it rent many of the older and bigger communities asunder. Men and women who had toiled together for years would not even speak to one another, and the only solution was separation.

The vast majority of the million new immigrants have turned their backs on the *kibbutz* in favour of more individualistic, even if co-operative forms of living. To the casual visitor there is little to distinguish Israel from other lands. There are cultural, colour and class distinctions. The rich grow richer and the poor grow poorer. When one penetrates below the surface one finds that the old ideals have not vanished, but the position is serious enough to make many wonder how far the existence of Israel is justified except as a home for those who were homeless.

If the thinking Israeli wonders to what unknown goal his land is moving, it is clear that the same doubts must in measure affect all thinking Jews for whom nationalism is a major factor in their outlook.

VI

THE JEW AND JESUS

THE shortness of this book makes it impossible to discuss at any length why the Jewish people did not accept Jesus. The New Testament makes it clear that they rejected Him, not because they were Jews, but because they were normal men and women. The greed and fears of the rulers, the vested interests and conservatism of the religious, the material hopes of the common people are all reflected in modern Christendom, where, by the majority, His name is mentioned with respect and His will spurned and ignored in daily life.

Paul goes further. In three chapters of agonized argument (Rom. 9–11) he makes clear that behind the rejection, *antedating it and causing it*, is God's action, God's " mystery " (Rom. 11 : 25), by which " a hardening in part hath befallen Israel until . . ." The main instruments which God used seem to have been the Jew's misunderstanding of his election and of the purpose of the Law, and these are operative to this day.

No Jew who has remained outside the Church has shown a deeper respect for Jesus of Nazareth than Sholem Asch.[1] In *My Personal Faith* he writes (pp. 106 *seq*), " What was quite new in the teaching of Jesus was that for the first time there appeared in Israel a teacher who, while in agreement with the law of Moses, did not derive his authority from that law. . . . He appealed to an authority which had been entrusted to his keeping.

---

[1] See especially his trilogy, *The Nazarene, The Apostle, Mary*.

... The Jews were bound to the authority which had been given to Moses on Sinai, and which they had recognized with their promise of obedience. They could not pass to the new authority without the sign which should proclaim that the old had been cancelled and the new one validated. ... The first coming of the Messiah was not for us but for the Gentiles."

Rabbi Klausner has written in his *Jesus of Nazareth* the first serious study of the life of Jesus in Hebrew. The final eight chapters (Eighth Book) are largely a vindication of the Jewish rejection of Jesus. One quotation must suffice. " In the self-same moment he both annulled *Judaism* as the *life-force* of the Jewish nation, and also the nation itself as a nation. ... This inevitably brought it to pass that his people, Israel, rejected him. ... Two thousand years of non-Jewish Christianity have proved that the Jewish people did not err " (pp. 390 f.).

But we must beware of exaggeration. The complete Jewish rejection of Jesus only began when the Church began to misinterpret Him. The first Church in Jerusalem consisted to a man of Jews, and there is not a church mentioned in Acts that did not have Jewish members. More than that: virtually all of the first generation of non-Jewish converts will have been influenced by the Synagogue before they heard the fuller truth from Christian missionaries, in most cases converted Jews.

The efforts by some in the Church of Jerusalem to enforce the keeping of the Law by Gentiles set up a certain tension. When the Church of Jerusalem was seriously weakened by the destruction of the city and Temple in 70 and irretrievably scattered after the collapse of Bar Cochba's revolt in 135, the predominantly Gentile churches were quick to forget their debt to the

Jewish Christians. The Jews, who had excommunicated the Jewish Christians, about A.D. 90, and had come to regard them as national traitors, when they refused to support Bar Cochba (after all he had proclaimed himself as the Messiah !), are not likely to have overlooked this lack of sympathy any more than they will have failed to draw their own conclusions from Marcion's denial in Rome (before 150) that the Old Testament was a divine revelation or of authority in the Church.

The weakened groups of Jewish Christians in Palestine and Syria, feeling themselves abandoned by their non-Jewish brothers, slid rapidly into heresy. Though they did not finally disappear until the Muslim conquest, they ceased to have any influence after 200. With them vanished the bridge between the Church and the Synagogue. Very soon we find the fantastic policy being adopted of demanding from the convert from Judaism that he renounce his Jewish heritage bag and baggage. The result was that the steady trickle of converts down the centuries, genuine and forced, never gave the Church a footing within Jewry. It is only in our own time that the Hebrew Christian movement has reversed this policy and is gradually making Jewry realize that a man can be both Jew and Christian.

The Church not only broke down its bridges with the past ; it rapidly built up a doctrinal wall of separation that effectively made it impossible for the Jew to recognize the Jesus of the Gospels.

Quite naturally, the Jew denied that the Church was the new people of God, but that was no justification for the Christian's affirming that the Jews had ceased to be the people of God. This attitude is seen in *The Epistle of Barnabas* (before 100) and the reasonably polite

THE JEW AND JESUS

Dialogue with Trypho by Justin Martyr (c. 160) and may be found all too often even today. Elliott-Binns is quite fair, when he says, "The Gentile Christian was, above all, anxious to show that there was nothing Jewish about him."[1]

It may seem obvious to us that the early Greek converts to Christianity should have had a strongly intellectual approach to their new faith, but "very early in the history of the Church . . . the idea arose under the influence of Greek philosophy that the divine revelation in the Bible had to do with the communication of those doctrinal truths which were inaccessible by themselves to human reason; and correspondingly that faith consisted in holding these supernaturally revealed doctrines for truth."[2] So Christianity became a type of religion alien both to Judaism and to the Old Testament. If the Jew tried to understand this new faith, he saw not the Man of Galilee but a figure set beside the one true God and denying His unity. This impression was intensified by the growing use of picture and image, which convinced the Jews that Christians were idolaters as well as polytheists.

The acceptance of a double standard of behaviour for Christians and the steady fall in that expected from the ordinary Church member, once the Church had become dominant in the Empire, led the Jew to realize that he was normally a more moral man than his 'Christian' neighbour—something that holds good today also. As a result he became convinced that the Christian attitude towards the Law was fundamentally false. He judged the tree by its fruit and condemned it.

[1] *The Beginnings of Western Christendom*, p. 82.
[2] Emil Brunner: *The Divine-Human Encounter*, p. 12.

When we realize that true faith is the result of God's personal revealing of Himself to man, we also realize that man's intellect is only one of the many factors that combine to decide whether a man will trust or continue in his rebellion. In other words, we shall feel sorrow rather than condemnation when nominal Christian or Jew, Muslim or pagan, turns his back on Jesus the Lord. Where, however, we are under the thrall of the old intellectual conception of religion and think that Christianity can be demonstrated to be true and the best of religions, we are always open to the temptation to think that those who reject it do so out of ill-will and deep-rooted evil. This has been the typical attitude of the Church from at least the time of Chrysostom (347-407), and *perfidia* became a standard word in the West to describe the Jew. Having thus arbitrarily established the ill-faith of the Jew, it was only a short step to deduce the crimes that such men would commit. It has been these arbitrary and imaginary crimes which anti-Judaism and anti-Semitism have battened on through the centuries and for which Jews have been murdered, robbed, expelled and reviled—all in the name of Christ!

In all centuries there have been Jews who have found their way to Jesus in spite of this barrier of false theology and false living. With some it has been the story of the New Testament that has done the work; with most it has been the realization of what Christianity can and should be, when they saw its outworking in the lives of true Christians. Paradoxically enough, it has been modern doubt and scepticism that has made it possible for the modern educated Jew to look anew at Jesus. In measure, as modern liberal secularism has forced the Church to climb from its pedestal and speak with a new humility, the Jew has felt that he was no longer compromising himself by reading the New Testament. The founding of the State of Israel has intensified this attitude, for here the Jew feels himself master in his own house. The number of conversions to Christianity still remains marginal, though much larger than most realize. Few would write or think of Him as did Sholem Asch. But though He is neither Messiah nor Saviour, and still less God to them, one can increasingly hear the Jew say, especially in Israel, " He is one of us". There are not a few who acknowledge that the Synagogue must learn from Him, but there are still few Christians willing to learn from the Synagogue.

In case a wrong impression has been created, it should be stressed that the Orthodox in Israel are increasingly exercising pressure on missions and Hebrew Christians. The majority of the population approved of the decision of the High Court stating that Father Daniel could not be regarded as a Jew, although he had been a convinced and active Zionist before his conversion, and he had repeatedly risked his life to rescue Polish Jews from the clutches of the Nazis. Israel may be prepared to welcome Jesus, but not yet the Jew who believes in Him.

VII

THE JEW AND I

IN this chapter I am assuming that you, who have read so far, and I are one in one outstanding fact; we have both found God and all His riches in Jesus Christ, and so we both trust and obey Him (the meaning of 'faith' in the New Testament). We may differ in the way we found Jesus, or rather were found by Him, and in the words we use to express our experience. We may also differ in the way we give expression to our gratitude, but we are agreed that we wish that all could share in our experience.

I imagine we agree too that ours is an experience that a man cannot be forced into and we deplore the many efforts in the past to compel the nonconformist, the Jew and the heretic to line up with the majority. Our own experience should convince us that it needed more than our brains to bring us where we now are, and so though we may be willing to indulge in a little argument with others, we realize that this will not be enough to bring them to share the riches that are ours. Their 'obtuseness' will not make us angry with them or make us unwilling to call them friends, though we shall be sorry, when we see them miss the best because they do not know Jesus as the Lord of life.

But what of the Jew we meet? There is in most of us an instinctive jealousy which shows itself whenever we find people claiming privilege because of accident of birth. Much of the dislike of the Jews can be traced to their claim to have been chosen by God. I must learn to realize that God chose this people for the good of mankind, and that His complete revelation of Himself up to its climax in Jesus Christ came through it. I must further accept that even their rejection of Jesus was God-willed for the sake of mankind (Rom. 11 : 11, 12, 28) and that their present hardening will have an end in God's good time (Rom. 11 : 26). This should create in me a sense of deep gratitude to God for the election and preservation of this people and a longing that they should share in the riches that have come to me through them.

But then the anti-Semite comes with his sweeping condemnations of the Jews, whom he regards as the refuse of the earth, or the poll-parrot repeats his words. Even if this were all true, the man who has discovered the true meaning of sin at the Cross is not likely to start constructing a scale of human sinfulness. The best answer, however, is to ask the anti-Semite and his poll-parrots for evidence. The latter will, of course, have none. The former may be relying on some forged document like *The Protocols of the Elders of Zion*, which would be mildly funny, if it had not deluded so many who were already emotionally ready to be convinced and through them led to the death and suffering of millions. But when we get past forgeries and fake passages from the Talmud and "everybody knows", we find that his evidence boils down to "I know two bad Jews, and all Jews are the same". The obvious answer is, "I know two bad Englishmen (or whatever the apposite nationality may be) and all Englishmen are the same!" Though the Jews show the faults and merits of other peoples—though not always in the same proportions—they tend to stand higher rather than lower. It is a great tribute to Judaism and an evidence of the grace of God at work that the long centuries of persecution and degradation so little influenced the moral fibre of Jewry.

When I come to know a Jew, I must be prepared to say to him as occasion serves, My people has sinned, My Church has sinned, and, it may well be, I have sinned, where the Jew is concerned. If I am concerned with justifying the past, even in part, then the Jew will seek to justify the past also, and the past will divide us, and we shall never get to the present and our riches that we wish to share.

However little I may like it, the Jew believes quite correctly that he has riches he can share with me, and he is not likely to want to hear of mine, unless I sincerely wish to know his. Normally, controversy between rival faiths runs along well-beaten paths. I present Christianity, or my particular form of it in an idealized form ; I forget all its many manifestations which have been sub-Christian or even un-Christian. On the other hand, I look for all the weaknesses of the rival faith, seeking to make it clear that no objective man can doubt where the superiority lies. My opponent knows that even if I have been objectively accurate, which is unlikely, yet I have not been fair. When I speak with a Jew, he has so consistently experienced the sub-Christian levels of Christianity, and the Church has so consistently devoted itself to the unworthy levels of Judaism, that only debate but not conversation is possible on the old paths.

True conversation with the Jew implies that I have realized that the only riches worth my bringing to him are Jesus Christ. It is based on the faith that however justly the Jew may be able to criticize the Church's history and perversions of Biblical teaching, however much he may reveal to me treasures in the Synagogue I never dreamt were there, yet Jesus Christ will remain so uniquely great to me that my faith in Him will not be shaken, but will rather be enriched, and in the end my Jewish friend will be moved " to jealousy " (Rom. 11 : 11).

The greatest wrong the Church ever did to Judaism was to punish the Christian converted to Judaism and his converter by death. It was the Church's supreme confession of its own weakness. When the Church realizes that as a human organization it is under the judgment of God, as are all human organizations, secular or religious, it will care little for the judgment of man. It will care equally little for proclaiming that which it knows to be under God's judgment, namely its own systems, and will be content to proclaim its Lord. If in the process it loses a few of its marginal members to those systems it approaches, it will be a small price, if Jesus Christ can once again be seen in His glory instead of in the ecclesiastical fog that has hidden Him from so many.

The millions of words of spoken and written debate with the Synagogue have done little to win Jews for Christ, though they may have served to arouse interest or to clinch matters for a will half won. In almost every case of genuine conversion the arresting and drawing power has been the vision of New Testament love (*agape*) as it is described in 1 Cor. 13 and as it has been lived in some Christian life, especially when it was realized that it marked not merely an individual but also the Church to which he belonged. The chief and unimportant exception to this is the Jew brought up in surroundings in which the prevailing ethos was Christian rather than Jewish.

It is entirely consistent with this that the biggest obstacle for many Jews when they face Jesus is not the tragic past, but the tragic divisions of the Church in the present. The discerning Jew sees in them the supreme denial of that love that had drawn him to the threshold of faith. The tragic history of their relationships has only underlined that Church and Synagogue belong inescapably together. In his persecution of the Jew Hitler was preparing his assault on the Church. In measure as the Church rediscovers that she is the Body of the Christ, i.e. of the Messiah, the Jew will discover that Jesus is his Messiah. But ultimately what the Church is depends on what you and I its members are. It is as we reflect the mercy shown to us that the Jew will also now obtain mercy (cf. Rom. 11 : 31 R.V.).

GLOSSARY

ANTI-SEMITISM. In Europe the justification for the dislike, hatred and persecution of the Jew had been sought virtually entirely on religious grounds. With the growth of liberal humanism in the nineteenth century some other justification was sought and was found in the alleged *racial* inferiority of the Semites—understand Jews, for it was never applied to the Arabs or other Semitic peoples. The term was first used in Germany in 1879 and spread rapidly, Austria, France and Russia being particularly influenced.

ARYAN. The Sanskrit-speaking invaders of North India in the first millennium B.C. spoke of themselves as *arya*, i.e. noble. Last century the term Aryan became used as a general name for the family of languages covering most of Europe and much of the western half of Asia. With the rise of anti-Semitism (*q.v.*), it became increasingly used for whatever racial group was being exalted as noble in contrast to the debased Semite. In fact, just as Semite has been made to equal Jew, so Aryan in this context generally equals German.

CHASSIDISM. In most mysticism (*q.v.*), the system is thought of as intended for those with special gifts, or able to devote much time to spiritual exercises. Its founder, Israel ben Eliezer (1700–1760), a natural mystic with a deep sympathy for the poverty which surrounded him and in which he shared, taught that piety was superior to scholarship. Since God infused all creation—he was on the verge of Pantheism, but did not cross the line—everyone, however poor and ignorant, could serve Him with every bodily function, so long as he served Him with joy and gladness.

GEMARA. A running commentary on the Mishnah (*q.v.*), written mainly in Aramaic. Unlike the Mishnah, which is mainly *halakah*, i.e. legal precept, it contains much *haggadah*, i.e. instructive stories, etc. The standard Gemara was compiled as the result of three centuries of discussion in the rabbinic schools of Babylonia, and was virtually complete by A.D. 500. The incomplete Palestinian version does not go much later than A.D. 300.

GHETTO. Both in the classic period and during the Dark Ages it was considered natural that an alien group like the Jews should live in its own district in a city. This was intensified by the canon of the Third Lateran Council of 1179 which forbade Jews and Christians to live together. This was never universally enforced, but as the Middle Ages drew to an end compulsory Jewish districts became commoner. The name is derived from the Jewish district in Venice set up in 1516. Ghettoes were very often surrounded by a wall with gates, which were locked at night. Today the term is often used of a district where Jews have continued to live, though they are free to move anywhere.

JEW-BADGE. The Fourth Lateran Council of 1215, not content with the ghetto system (*q.v.*), tried to enforce the separation of Jew and Christian by making the former wear a hat or badge of distinctive colour, sometimes red but generally yellow. This law was only consistently enforced from the sixteenth century. It was one of the customs revived by Hitler, who made all Jews wear a yellow star of David.

JUDAISM. The religion of the Jews. It is normally not applied to the period before the destruction of the Temple (A.D. 70), except to those phenomena that were developed later.

KIBBUTZ. The usual name given to a communal agricultural settlement in Israel. The main features of a *kibbutz* are: (1) The property of the community is owned equally by all adult members of the community. (2) Though normal family life exists within the community, every fit adult works for the community, not his family, and so the community bears corporate responsibility for the upbringing of

GLOSSARY

the children. (3) All work is shared among all members of the community and no hired workers are used. In recent years there has been some tendency to modify these principles, especially the last, for special gifts are now commonly recognized.

KABBALISM. Kabbala or Cabbala means tradition. It is the form of Jewish mysticism (*q.v.*) best known outside Jewry, at least by repute. Its chief work is the *Zohar* (thirteenth century), which is in theory a commentary on the Pentateuch. The concept is that the minutiae of Scripture are capable of leading into mystic knowledge of the nature of God and of the origin of the universe and man. Outside Jewry it was often thought to be a system of magic.

MESSIAH. Though there have been currents within Judaism, which have looked on the Messiah as more than man, though not as divine, the predominant view regarded him as being purely a man. Hence it was easy for outstanding figures to obtain recognition in wide circles as the Messiah. The two best known pseudo-Messiahs are Bar Kochba, who led the last great rebellion against Rome (132-135), and Sabbatai Zevi (1626-1676). The great hopes and even greater disappointment caused by the latter partly explain the widespread tendency of the modern Jew to regard the Messiah merely as the personification of a time of final blessing.

MIDRASH. Pl. Midrashim. During the period of the compilation of the Talmud (*q.v.*) commentaries on the books of the Old Testament came into being, which to this day are authoritative for Orthodox Jews.

MISHNAH. The earlier part of the Talmud (*q.v.*). It may be regarded as a commentary on the legal portions of the Pentateuch (*q.v.*) or as a codification of the Oral Law (*q.v.*). Though many parts are older, it took its final form about A.D. 200. It is written in Hebrew.

MYSTICISM. A term used for a phenomenon in all developed religions, for man's enjoyment, or attempt at enjoyment, of direct fellowship with and knowledge of the Deity. Since it is used for as wide a range of experience as that of St Paul to followers of the Hindu Upanishads, great care must be taken to understand how any individual author uses it. It is to be noted that the influence of the Old Testament was strong enough to keep Jewish mysticism from slipping into the pantheism which is such a marked feature of its eastern and Islamic forms.

ORAL LAW. In the inter-testamental period, i.e. after the return from the exile in Babylonia, those who wished to bring the people completely under the control of the Mosaic Law found that in many cases a traditional interpretation of certain laws already existed, and certain customs, like the washing of hands, were observed that were not expressly commanded in the Law. This interpretation and these customs form the basis of the Oral Law, which was steadily enlarged until it took definitive form in the Mishnah (*q.v.*). In fact anything not made completely clear there or in the Gemara (*q.v.*) has been further clarified down to our own day. The Oral Law is of equal authority for the Orthodox with the Pentateuch (*q.v.*), and its beginnings are attributed to Moses.

PENTATEUCH. The five books of Moses, Genesis to Deuteronomy. The common Jewish name is Torah (*q.v.*). It is considered by the Orthodox that it is a transcript of a heavenly original, and therefore its authority is higher than that of the other Old Testament books.

RABBI. See footnote, p. 24. The term 'the rabbis' is often used, where the context suits, of the great teachers in the formative period of Judaism.

RABBINIC JUDAISM. The Judaism presented to us in the Talmud (*q.v.*) and the Midrashim (*q.v.*).

GLOSSARY

SYNAGOGUE. In its inception the Synagogue was as much a community house and a house of study as a place of worship. Under Christian influence Synagogue is like Church used both for the spiritual society and the building.

TALMUD. This is found in two, somewhat divergent forms, the Palestinian and the fuller and authoritative Babylonian. It is composed of the Mishnah (*q.v.*) which is common to both, and the Gemara (*q.v.*). It is the official exposition of the Oral Law (*q.v.*) and in addition throws a flood of light on the views of Rabbinic Judaism.

TORAH. The Divine Instruction, normally but inadequately rendered Law. It may mean according to context, the Pentateuch (*q.v.*), the laws contained in it, or the Pentateuch and Talmud (*q.v.*) together, i.e. the written ' Law ' and its traditional exposition.

ZIONISM. Though the hope of return to Palestine never died in Jewry, it was normally a religious hope, generally linked with the coming of the Messiah. The movement started by Theodor Herzl in 1896–7 (see p. 20) was an avowed attempt to solve the Jewish problem by secular means. Though it has its strongly religious wing, the Zionist movement has always remained true to its secular vision.

Statistics of JEWISH POPULATIONS in 1927 and 1957

		1927	1957
EUROPE.	British Isles	310,000	455,500
	Holland	110,000	22,000
	Belgium	50,000	33,000
	France	155,000	300,000
	Italy	72,000	32,000
	Switzerland	21,000	19,000
	Scandinavia	15,500	22,300
	Germany	550,000	27,300
	Czecho-Slovakia	360,000	17,000
	Austria	350,000	10,000
	Hungary	500,000	155,000
	Yugoslavia	65,000	6,500
	Turkey	168,000	62,000
	Roumania	950,000	200,000
	U.S.S.R.	3,160,000	3,000,000
	Poland	2,870,000	45,000
	Other Countries	594,000	19,200
N. AMERICA	Canada	160,000	233,000
	U.S.A.	3,750,000	5,433,000
SOUTH AND CENTRAL AMERICA		175,000	767,200
ASIA	Palestine (Israel)	160,000	1,750,000
	Arab Countries	152,000	48,000
	Persia	50,000	75,000
	Other Countries	204,500	30,500
AFRICA.	North	600,000	425,000
	Central and South	104,500	137,600
AUSTRALASIA		25,500	61,500
		15,682,000	13,386,600

The figures for 1927 are taken from *The Christian Approach to the Jew* (Conference Report, E.H.P. 1927), corrected in the light of later knowledge; those for 1957 are taken from *The Jewish Year Book*. It should be borne in mind that most are approximations. Those for the U.S.A. are probably an underestimate, those for the U.S.S.R. (1957) almost certainly an overestimate.

By 1962 the Jewish population of Israel had passed two millions.

BOOKS FOR FURTHER READING

A standard work covering much of this study is
J. Jocz: *The Jewish People and Jesus Christ* (S.P.C.K.)
but you are likely to find it far too detailed except for reference.

CHAPTER II

James Parkes: *A History of the Jewish People* (Weidenfeld and Nicolson). A brilliant survey of all the main movements in Jewish history.

Cecil Roth: *A Short History of the Jewish People* (East and West Library). This combines the features of being reasonably short and yet adequate in its presentation of the subject.

James Parkes: *Antisemitism* (Valentine Mitchell). A study by the greatest living authority on the subject.

CHAPTER III

W. N. Carter: *Sons of the Law* (The Church's Ministry among the Jews). An elementary introduction to Judaism and Jewish life with the advantage of dealing with matters often taken for granted in bigger works.

I. Epstein: *Judaism* (Epworth Press). A clearly written study by an outstanding Jewish scholar.

I. Epstein: *Judaism* (Pelican Books). A condensed historical presentation.

M. Waxman: *Judaism—Religion and Ethics* (Yoseloff). A rather fuller but fundamentally simple presentation of Judaism in all its aspects.

C. G. Montefiore and H. Loewe: *A Rabbinic Anthology* (Macmillan). Classical Judaism is allowed to speak for itself through a carefully chosen and arranged selection of passages from the Talmud and other writings of the same period. Comments by a Liberal and an Orthodox scholar throw light on modern Judaism.

A. Cohen: *Everyman's Talmud* (Dent). A well-balanced and interestingly written guide to the contents of the Talmud.

CHAPTER IV

H. M. Sachar: *The Course of Modern Jewish History* (Weidenfeld and Nicholson). An invaluable reference book for the history of the Jew since the French Revolution.

N. Bentwich: *The Jews in Our Time* (Pelican Books). A picture of contemporary Jewry in brief compass.

A. Lukyn Williams: *The Doctrines of Modern Judaism Considered* (S.P.C.K.). An acute and sympathetic study written before nationalism had gained its present importance.

I. I. Mattuck: *The Essentials of Liberal Judaism* (Routledge). The author was for many years an unquestioned leader of Liberal Judaism in Britain.

CHAPTER V

Chaim Weizmann: *Trial and Error* (Hamish Hamilton). The growth and triumph of Zionism as seen by one of the main actors in it.

S. Perowne: *The One Remains* (Hodder & Stoughton). An attempt at an unbiased picture of what the founding of the State of Israel has meant for the Arab refugees.

BOOKS FOR FURTHER READING

CHAPTER VI

Lev Gillet : *Communion in the Messiah* (Lutterworth Press). A most sympathetic study from the Christian side.

CHAPTER VII

G. Hedenquist : *The Church and the Jewish People* (Edinburgh House Press). A symposium dealing with various aspects of the subject.

A number of these works are out of print, but should be obtainable in libraries. Many contain valuable bibliographies. Details about the Jewish Community in Great Britain can be best obtained from the current volume of *The Jewish Year Book*.